Managing People and Situations

© **Coachwise** Ltd and Sports Officials UK (SOUK), 2005

ISBN-13: 978-1-902523-97-0
ISBN-10: 1-902523-97-0

Author
Professor Craig Mahoney

SOUK Review Group
Stuart Cummings, Russell D'Costa, Janie Frampton, Dr David Pegg

Editor
Aislinn Kelly

Assistant Editor
Craig Smith

Designer
Saima Nazir

Photographs courtesy of actionplus unless otherwise stated.

For further information on SOUK, please visit www.sportsofficialsuk.com

Published by

Coachwise

Coachwise Ltd
Chelsea Close
Off Amberley Road
Armley
Leeds LS12 4HP
Tel: 0113-231 1310
Fax: 0113-231 9606
Email: enquiries@coachwise.ltd.uk
Website: www.coachwise.ltd.uk

Designed and produced by **Coachwise Business Solutions**, a brand of **Coachwise** Ltd

050223

If you wish to publish some material for your organisation, please contact us at enquiries@coachwisesolutions.co.uk
If you are an author and wish to submit a manuscript for publication, please contact us at enquiries@1st4sport.com

About the Author and SOUK Review Group

The author, **Professor Craig Mahoney**, is a squash referee who has officiated at national and international tournaments. He has a PhD in sport psychology and worked with the English Premier League officials as their professional sport psychologist between 2001 and 2005. Craig has worked with officials in ice and field hockey and ran psychology seminars for the International Cricket Council's full-time professional umpires and referees prior to 2004's ICC Trophy in England. He is also currently a Professor at the University of Wolverhampton.

Stuart Cummings achieved senior referee status in 1991 and was appointed as the Match Officials Director at The Rugby Football League in 2002. During his refereeing career, he refereed six test matches, two World Cup finals, four Challenge Cup finals and two Grand finals.

Former national-level men's gymnastics judge in Australia, **Russell D'Costa** worked as a Coaching and Officiating Consultant with the Australian Sports Commission before accepting a position in the UK as an Education and Training Manager at sports coach UK. He is now a Senior Project Officer, coaching and officiating development with the Office for Recreation and Sport in Adelaide, South Australia.

As a referee, **Janie Frampton** has reached the National List of Contributory League and Women's National Premier League football. She is a qualified UEFA B Coach, FA Licensed Referee Instructor, FA Generic Tutor Trainer, Tutor Mentor for Child Protection and an FA Regional Referee Manager.

Dr David Pegg has experience as an international badminton umpire and has officiated at many World, European, All-England and National Championships. He is also an international referee, organising events both in England and overseas.

Managing People and Situations

Contents

Managing People and Situations

Chapter 1

Managing People and Situations – Where Do We Start?

Introduction

Sports officiating is becoming an increasingly popular activity for those with the skills, passion and ability to succeed as officials. In many sports, the introduction of professionalism has brought new career opportunities, with well-paid performers in many sports, massive endorsement opportunities and a range of other benefits arising from the sometimes large sources of money associated with sport. The range of sports that offer fantastic financial rewards is often linked with television rights and include cricket, darts, football, golf, ice hockey, motor racing, rugby league, rugby union, snooker, squash and tennis. Some of these sports have also introduced professional or semi-professional officials to oversee the rules or laws of the sport (some sports use one term, some the other; we shall use rules/laws as general designation). This is in order to establish a credible, impartial evaluation of the sporting performance.

Within such sports, the concept of paid officials, a career structure and promotion potential are now strongly embedded in the thinking and development of governing bodies. However, some may still wonder why anyone would pursue an interest in becoming sports officials. Performers, coaches, fans and the media love to hate them. However, they remain a fundamental part of sport. The key attributes required to become a top official in a chosen sport are as diverse and difficult to achieve as those required to become an outstanding sports performer. Determination, commitment, skill, ability and intelligence are needed to reach elite sport status; those wanting to become top sports officials also require these characteristics.

Depending upon the sport, officials will need a range of physical and technical skills: these are almost identical for any official performing at the highest level. However, the mental skills and abilities that top officials demonstrate will be the determining factor between those who reach the highest levels and those who don't. Just as knowing the rules of the road does not mean you can drive well, knowing the rules/laws of the game does not mean you can officiate effectively, with the right level of understanding, awareness and experiential knowledge to manage the people and situations that will impact on all competitive playing arenas. It is therefore essential that officials work to optimise their skills, including the mental aspects that an official will be expected to develop to the highest possible standard.

Psychology has been used for centuries to understand, support and develop the behaviour and cognitive (mental) abilities of humans. However, only since the late 1970s has any real emphasis been given to how this same knowledge can be used to assist performers in sport. The initial thrust came from the Eastern European nations, who sought respect and recognition of their political regimes through sport. Sports governing bodies in these countries looked to understand their respective sports by applying more than just skill development programmes, which gave heightened interest to physiology, psychology, biomechanics and medicine. Soon after, the Americans, Canadians and Australians began to appreciate the added benefits of applying science to sport. They invested heavily in research and application of many of the Olympic-based sports that the Eastern Europeans were beginning to excel in by this point.

The use of sport psychology has increased considerably over recent years and this has now been more widely accepted across all aspects of sport: not just by the performers, but also the support staff and, now, the officials. The skills required to manage sporting competitions will be determined by a combination of mental (cognitive) and behavioural (somatic) abilities. The development of physical and technical ability is often well documented and generally accepted by sports performers. However, the use, development and integration of the mental aspects of sport are less well understood. At World, Olympic or Commonwealth level, the difference between winning and losing will not usually be a result of physical or technical ability – since both of these are so well known and developed, the differences at the top are almost indistinguishable – but are usually in the mental skills, ability and toughness of those coming first, second or third. This includes how sports performers manage the people and situations in which they find themselves.

Many people involved in sport are fearful of psychology, believing that it represents a weakness in their makeup and that, to talk about psychology, seek support from a psychologist or suggest that psychology is a fundamental need within their sport, is to risk ridicule from friends or colleagues. However, far from being apprehensive about sport psychology, everyone involved in sport should feel excited about adding this *final* dimension to their preparation. Sport psychology is about the cognitive and somatic aspects of performance, as it relates to practice, performance or competition. The role of a sport psychologist is to support performers, coaches, managers and officials in optimising their mental and behavioural skills in order to produce continual peak performances.

Alan Edwards

Since the early 1970s, the use of science in sport has resulted in major advances in our understanding of what is required to produce sporting excellence in most sports. This has also led to acknowledgement that different requirements arise for elite performance across sports but, even at development stages, the demands placed on children or adults (males or females, abled or disabled) will vary. This differentiation in need has enabled scientists and coaches to work closely together to provide the best support programmes possible and a wonderful opportunity for the 1980s European ideal *Sport for All* to be more easily accomplished.

In reference to psychology in sport, considerable interest has been generated in the last 20 years, since medal winners in major competitions have differentiated their performances in finals not on their technical or physical ability (both of which are deemed to be almost identical at the highest level) but on their mental toughness, which is seen to be the deciding factor between winners and losers in major competition finals. And, while the sports performers themselves have received considerable interest from sport psychologists, coaches, managers and officials, officials have had relatively little attention paid to them. More recently, it has been recognised that officials experience a range of mental demands that are a combination of those similar to that of a performer but also others that are vastly different, arguably more intense, less easy to resolve and that demand considerable time, effort, mental energy and support.

This resource is designed to give an insight into some of the demands of managing people and situations as an official, regardless of level, but to also help officials prepare to be the best they can in this competitive, stressful and exciting domain of sport. The concept of managing people and situations is not about lying on a couch and talking to a psychologist; it is about the real management issues that affect all officials who have direct contact with performers in their sports. It covers the professional preparation of officials, including controlling the environment and spectators, managing conflict and injury, communication strategies, being aware of how decision-making processes will be adversely affected by the game and developing strategies to deal with the many and varied pressures of being an official.

The Experience Account

Perhaps the most valuable attribute possessed by any official is experience. Experience arises from being involved in and building awareness of situations. This can happen by actually doing the work, reading about the work or observing others doing the work. However, *doing* is always better than reading or observing. As experience builds, in the same way as money is saved in a bank account, officials can build the valuable officiating knowledge they need to succeed in an *experience account*. An *experience account* is a figure of speech that illustrates the amount of officiating and training experience that has been built up over an officiating career and can be topped up by training, education and officiating.

Every time officials train or officiate, they make deposits into their experience accounts. It is also useful for officials to reinforce their training and officiating by making notes in a logbook, recording what they have learned from their officiating. In this way, they can look back at their logbook, see what they have learned and build up a reserve of experience that they can call upon when needed (eg what works, what fails, the adverse situations they have overcome, positive experiences they have had, examples of good practice).

However, when officials look for shortcuts or skip some vital areas of their training in order to save time and effort, their experience account can become overdrawn. Here, their experience level would be lower than the level of competition in which they are officiating so, if a large reserve of experience is not sustained by continually making deposits, by training and by officiating at a higher standard, they can end up being overdrawn in competition. This is very similar to the principle of overload used to prepare the physical development of performers.

Perhaps the most difficult issue to resolve for any official is how to develop the skills and abilities that will help them to be decisive but consistent, calm yet confident, assertive while developing a rapport with the performers, and that will demonstrate integrity, judgement and clarity. It is also essential that officials are able to feel some level of enjoyment from the role as, just as performers will stop competing if enjoyment diminishes, officials will also withdraw themselves from involvement if the experience is overly stressful, lacks enjoyment or fails to provide them with a personal satisfaction commensurate with the effort involved.

The Skill Toolkit

To be an official in sport requires, as a minimum, that the official knows the rules/laws of the sport in such a manner as to necessitate little logical intervention to the decision-making process. This is known as automation or tacit response and will be ever-present in experienced, high-level officials who have seen most situations in previous competitions and, thus, have drawn almost innately on their experience accounts. To achieve this, officials must know the rules/laws and all possible interpretations in their totality. Officials need to have experienced the entire range of sporting circumstances and need to be confident at applying the rules/laws quickly, decisively and accurately.

The Skill Toolkit

Skills that will build resilience include:

- an in-depth knowledge of the rules/laws
- excellent and enhanced communication skills
- anxiety control strategies and awareness of anxiety
- the ability to monitor and control body language
- enhanced motivation, confidence and concentration
- imagery ability
- people-management skills
- the ability to read the play and feel the game
- highly developed anticipatory skills
- good mental toughness.

The Pressure Cooker

Being a sports official may often feel like being stuck in a pressure cooker. Long before the start of a sporting contest, sports officials will often be involved in the event preparation process, which may include resolving security issues, monitoring weather conditions, assessing playing surfaces and reviewing sporting implements. When the sporting contest finally begins, the viewing public is unlikely to appreciate the time, effort and resources required by officials just to get the competition underway. However, the viewing public is less concerned about the lead up to the event and is rather desperately keen to see a contest monitored and overseen by officials, though not one that is determined by the officials or where officials take the centre-stage position. It is particularly important that officials remain relatively *unobtrusive* throughout the contest, as this will ensure that the event develops its own momentum without the officials becoming the centre of attention or the recipient of anger and aggression from the performers, coaches, managers or spectators.

An Example from English Premier League Football

Officials are fundamental to most sports and are, arguably, the only impartial people associated with a competitive match. Professional officials, paid a stipend and match fee, have been a reality in the English Premier League for the past four seasons. A multi-million pound game is now managed and controlled by high-quality, professionally competent, highly skilled, physically fit and mentally tough officials with the support of three assistant officials.

Psychological support is now provided to the English Premier League referees who officiate in the Premier League and some of the more difficult Football League matches, and nine of these referees will also officiate in European domestic and National qualifiers or World Cup qualifying matches in the lead up to major annual or four-yearly championships. This support focuses on the mental and behavioural needs of officials. Support has been provided following an initial needs analysis, used to determine the baseline mental skill level, motivational needs and personal aspirations of each of the 20 referees in the Select Group (this group comprises the full-time professional referees in the English game who officiate at all the Premier League matches, some Football League matches and often the difficult derbies). Matchday routines, post-match activity and daily living requirements have been found to form a fundamental part of the support network required by referees and this has been identified as crucial to success, no matter at what level a referee operates.

Sport psychology has been used to help referees (and performers) develop consistent internal support systems to enhance mental and behavioral attributes that improve sporting performance. Analysis of the changes in mental and behavioural skills has clearly demonstrated that structured programmes of mental skills support, and personal development programmes have a positive impact on, refereeing performance. Officials need to be multi-skilled and should possess characteristics that enable them to maintain control over 22 performers, spectators, managers and substitutes while minimising the coercive influences from the spectators, performers, managers and support staff, during in-match decision-making.

Officials are typically sensitive people who internalise outcomes. They can be affected by spectators' reactions and interference, performers' abuse and managers' discontent. When officiating decisions are badly interpreted, they will sometimes process negative thoughts, which can interrupt thinking clarity. The control of unwanted thoughts using thought-stopping strategies is quite important when managing emotions, maintaining composure and keeping objectivity. The use of positive thinking and personal affirmations (eg 'I am the greatest') can be useful in helping this refocusing skill.

All officials need to understand their personal arousal needs if they are to optimise their performance and give the best they can. This includes having a clear set of short-, medium- and long-term goals, being able to motivate themselves (and their assistants) prior to, during and following games, regardless of weather, teams, venue, difficulty, outcome or insults. Goals should be Specific, Measurable, Agreed, Realistic and Time-phased (SMART). For example, 'today I will ensure my voice is crisp, that I give loud, clear decisions, that I minimise errors and give accurate timely decisions to minimise confusion.'

Within sport, performers and coaches usually believe officials perform below acceptable and expected standards (ie there is a high error rate). However, officials' confidence (in the Premier League) in their decisions is generally very high. This perceptual difference must be acknowledged and recognised if performers, managers and officials are to integrate their respective roles effectively.

To establish the correct mental state prior to performance, Premier League officials follow a typical and consistent match-preparation plan. This includes the team (four officials) meeting upto four hours before kick-off and beginning personal and collective preparation strategies, which incorporate a review of the teams, the ground, signalling, teamwork, physical states, mental states and situational warm-ups. For officials wanting to optimise their skills in officiating, give the teams they officiate their best performance and officiate the best they can, the words of Ayrton Senna da Silva (1960–94) may be useful: '...work...learn, learn fast if possible...be the best – the boldest – under all circumstances and never...stop progressing.'

The FA

Alan Edwards

Chapter 2

Managing People

Psychology

An official's job, first and foremost, is to take care of the game. An effective official must understand how to manage people. Officials have to manage performers, coaches, managers, spectators and fellow officials. There are a number of basic rules that apply to the management of people that are relevant to sport and to life. An official who is to manage people effectively will need to understand people's behaviour and needs. With pressures in officiating increasing, partly as a consequence of video technology, media interest, higher financial stakes and greater accountability, effective officials must be well organised and highly adept at understanding behaviour and needs in the sporting environment.

Most sports performers will adopt innate instinctive behaviours that they have learned during their sporting careers when they find themselves in unusual or difficult sporting situations. This can then produce emotional responses that may result in an official and a performer disagreeing. Such situations can quickly disintegrate if the official fails to manage the conditions effectively. Performers can be very quick to reach conclusions and may be subjective, which can generate negative feelings and insecurity. The management of people will be most effective for officials if they focus on positive aspects and behaviours by rewarding these and being clear, accurate and responsive to negative and inappropriate behaviour.

Understanding why people engage in competition will help officials to recognise the needs that have promoted this interest. Surveys on youth sport show that fun and enjoyment are the most significant factors associated with continued involvement and motivation. With age and the development of skill, the motivational factors may shift towards higher-level needs, including achievement, responsibility, recognition and money. If officials are aware of the needs that performers have from competition, they can at least understand some of the actions and reactions produced by them in competition.

An official's skill toolkit must involve communication skills. Effective managers should be able to listen carefully, interpret correctly and make use of conscious and unconscious physical movements (body language) to communicate thoughts, feelings and messages.

Performers will respond most positively to officials if they feel they can trust them and if they have confidence in the ability of the official. To achieve this, officials must provide opportunities to reduce insecurity in the minds of the performers. This is supported by officiating that encourages the demonstration of ability by enabling free-flowing play, where performer involvement and participation is optimised. Confidence is also enhanced by officials who are able to minimise fear. Fear will arise if performers are unable to understand the decision-making process that affects their game. Fear will be minimised if officials can gain the trust and respect of the performers. Neither of these attributes can be taken for granted and must be worked on intensively in order to achieve them.

Experienced officials also have a role in the management and development of other officials. Succession planning is a common phenomenon in corporate life; the same process is apparent in a sporting context, where teams often purchase replacement performers and new recruits to take the place of ageing performers as their careers progress. For experienced officials, the same opportunities arise as young, inspired individuals become committed to officiating when they see a colleague or work with a colleague for whom they have respect.

The most effective way for officials to manage that development process is to teach by example, acting as a role model to inspire others and provide an example of good practice. Sharing the skills, knowledge and abilities they have acquired throughout their careers is the most powerful management role they can play in the development of other officials. Often, this can be further supported by acting as a coach, mentor or counsellor to the aspirant young official. Even just spending time talking to them, answering their questions or listening to their experiences can be highly motivational.

Another important aspect of managing new and developing officials is to ensure the management of quality. An understanding of quality and standards is not purely developmental but must also be supported by an awareness of the minimum expectations. Knowing the rules/laws of the game does not, in itself, imply high quality or the maintenance of standards. Therefore, it is essential that succession planning of this sort is supported by new officials who are learning by experience but are being supported by a constant review and monitoring process. The momentum that will arise from continued improvement and the clear observation of improvement will also assist this development process.

Flow experience is about getting mentally *in the groove*. This happens when an official's energy is properly directed towards desired goals. These optimal experiences are produced by motivated people. Motivated people are those who feel valued and respected for what they do. Officials have a responsibility to respect performers, unless they give them cause to lose respect. However, this should not be carried forward to the next time they officiate the performers.

Managing Performers

Officials should:

- try to influence behaviour rather than change personalities

- encourage and reward constructive behaviour

- say *thank you* to people whenever it is merited

- allow people the opportunity to express themselves where appropriate

- practise reading body language

- give people clear messages.

Communication

Making oneself understood is one of the most difficult skills anyone can learn. Sociologists often consider language to be 'dangerous', particularly if it is used incorrectly or lacks sensitivity, or when little consideration is given to the manner in which it will be interpreted. Officials have a responsibility to ensure not only that they are understood but also that messages they send are received with due consideration to the sensitivities of those receiving them. In any sporting contest, without doubt, the performers should be the key personnel and, therefore, officials need to be careful not inadvertently to distract performers so they are unable to perform optimally. That is not to suggest that an official should be subservient or that an official should accept language or behaviour that is derogatory or disparaging to other performers, spectators, officials or support teams, or which contravenes the rules/laws of the game.

Communication is, of course, not just about verbal interaction. Officials will either knowingly or unknowingly use a variety of communication strategies when controlling a game (eg hand and arm signals, such as waving their hands, pointing their finger or gesturing continuous play). Such gestures are powerful in sports whether the official has an active role or is stationary.

RFU

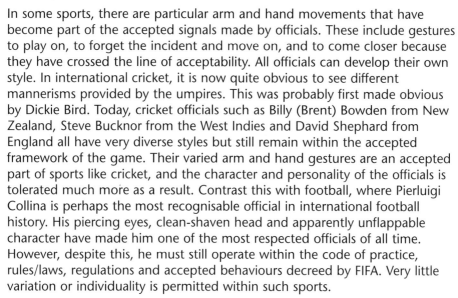

In some sports, there are particular arm and hand movements that have become part of the accepted signals made by officials. These include gestures to play on, to forget the incident and move on, and to come closer because they have crossed the line of acceptability. All officials can develop their own style. In international cricket, it is now quite obvious to see different mannerisms provided by the umpires. This was probably first made obvious by Dickie Bird. Today, cricket officials such as Billy (Brent) Bowden from New Zealand, Steve Bucknor from the West Indies and David Shephard from England all have very diverse styles but still remain within the accepted framework of the game. Their varied arm and hand gestures are an accepted part of sports like cricket, and the character and personality of the officials is tolerated much more as a result. Contrast this with football, where Pierluigi Collina is perhaps the most recognisable official in international football history. His piercing eyes, clean-shaven head and apparently unflappable character have made him one of the most respected officials of all time. However, despite this, he must still operate within the code of practice, rules/laws, regulations and accepted behaviours decreed by FIFA. Very little variation or individuality is permitted within such sports.

Clearly, the dilemma experienced by some officials is how to use their personality in a competitive arena without adversely altering the flow of the game or changing the way in which performers can perform to their best. The role of the official is to exercise control by applying the rules/laws governing the sport, whether that is the international governing body or, as in some sports, the local interpretation of those international rules/laws.

However, regardless of officials' personalities, their key roles are to maintain control of the performers, the game, the coaches/managers and the immediate viewing public. To do this, their management skills will be constantly tested and their ability to make use of the most widespread set of communication strategies will be a deciding factor in their success. Verbal communication is fundamental and hand and arm gestures are equally important. Body language is similarly appropriate but can be misinterpreted. While a comprehensive understanding of body language may not be necessary, it is essential to understand what body language is and what it can do. The body language of performers will alter when they make a mistake. Often, they will drop their shoulders, facial expressions of emotions will change (anger, fear, depression etc) and a feeling of lethargy can set in. True champions will hide this or make use of skills to cover the effects.

In tennis, Bjorn Borg was a wonderful example of a performer who could hide his feelings of anxiety, concern, fear and excitement until after the match had finished. His contemporary, John McEnroe, was quite different, allowing his verbal outbursts to inspire his own performance to new and higher levels. However, these are extremes and most performers and officials will respond very quickly with typical body language responses in a variety of situations. It is quite common for officials in some sports to become much quieter when they make a mistake or for their head and shoulders to droop forward when they know an error has occurred. In such circumstances, sensitive performers will look to exploit the situation, knowing the official has been compromised and may not be coping well. At this point, performers may try to increase the pressure on officials, asking for more decisions, seeking a more in-depth explanation, being more assertive, constantly talking to the official, reducing time and space for the official to recover composure and ensure a balanced and objective review of the situation.

Verbal Communication

Verbal communication will be the main form of communication with performers in any sport. In fact, in some sports, the only type of formal contact between the official and the performers will be the spoken word. It is therefore essential that the officials can be understood and that they respond in a calm yet controlled manner, exercise compassion in the way in which they communicate and, above all, take time to be understood. The latter will be particularly relevant when working with performers who speak a different language from the one the official is using. In such circumstances, officials will need to use all their skills to ensure they officiate correctly, exercising a range of communication options to maintain control.

Facial Expressions

It is possible to exhibit a range of expressions from the face that will enable performers to have a clear indication of the official's intentions. Anger can be clearly demonstrated by facial changes. So, too, can cheerfulness, which can imply that it is all going well and the official is delighted with the way the performers are responding to the enforcement of the rules/laws of the game. Confusion is also easily displayed by facial change and it is important that officials are careful about forming expressions that might imply they do not know what is going on, what has just happened or what the correct decision should be. Officials' personalities can often come through very strongly from facial gestures. Some officials will constantly talk to performers and use humour, signals of enjoyment and smiling to convey a sense of satisfaction and, by doing so, can defuse aggression from performers and situations.

Other officials will have more assertive personalities and will use this to manage the game. Whatever an official's personality, each official must make use of their knowledge, skills, ability and personality to optimise their officiating role, while not developing an over-inflated opinion of their relevance to the game and certainly not to the spectators.

Other expressions that can be used effectively as part of the officiating role include the simple smile, which can neutralise a difficult situation quickly and make performers feel at ease. Frowns can be interpreted as aggressiveness or uncertainty regarding a decision. It is essential that officials do not present mixed messages. It would be inappropriate for an official to issue a red card and expel a performer from the game while wearing a huge smile.

Body Language

What can officials do about body language? The most important first step for officials is to be aware of its existence and the impact it can have on them or those they are officiating. Officials must become aware of their own body movements, gestures they may overuse in pressurised situations, facial changes that imply they may have lost control and even voice pattern changes that arise when their somatic stress levels have increased. The best way for officials to monitor some of these is by having regular video reviews of their personal performances. If this does not systematically occur, they could ask a friend to set up a video camera so that they can see how they behave, providing this is acceptable within the sport's policies and procedures.

The impact that body language will have is very powerful. Most people will be aware of the closed nature and defensiveness of a person crossing their arms or that standing with hands on hips implies readiness and aggression or that walking tall and upright signifies positivity and confidence. As soon as officials arrive at a venue, they may be observed by performers, spectators, managers and television crews (if appropriate). The manner in which an official uses posture and body language pre-game, during the game and post-game can give considerable cues to performers and teams looking to exploit any weaknesses they feel are evident. For example, officials who stand with their heads up, arms out by their sides and fists closed are presenting strong body language that can be interpreted as readiness for anything and confidence in their abilities.

Spatial Awareness

When officials communicate with performers in any sport, the use of their own personal space and the personal space of performers can significantly impact on how officials are received. The invasion of personal space is often intimidating and officials must be sensitive to the way they might unintentionally invade such spaces. For some cultures, this will lead to responses that can include unexpected aggression or subservience. Similarly, performers will try and invade the personal space of an official if they are confident, feel aggrieved and want to make a point.

The way personal space is managed will also be a measure of an official's skills. In football, officials will often separate performers from situations to talk with them independently. This management skill and communication strategy can work very effectively but can also be compromised by other performers choosing to follow the offending performer and remonstrate with the official. Officials must also be careful not to move around assertively, as taking up a lot of space can sometimes make performers feel threatened.

Hand Signals

Hand signals are a very powerful tool. Whether an officiating role involves sitting, standing or running with the play, the use of hand, arm and leg gestures can be an effective tool to alert performers to what needs to happen next. In some sports, such as cricket, the use of hands, arms and legs is part of the official signalling duties of the umpire. However, in other sports, custom and practice has led to some unofficial signals being incorporated into the game, which have added useful support to the normal officiating role (eg pointing to the service box to be used next in squash or signalling to play on by raising arms together in netball or football). Similarly, raising one finger to the mouth to alert a performer to say nothing more or they are likely to be disciplined, or gesturing a performer to come over because the official wants to speak with them, or directing them off the field because they have been dismissed, are equally powerful non-verbal communication skills that officials can use to enhance effectiveness.

Eye Contact

The use of eye contact with performers is extremely important. Many performers will struggle to maintain eye contact when they are being disciplined. This is usually because they know they have been caught doing something wrong and so behave with some childlike responses. However, at times, it is useful to avoid *full-on* eye contact, as it can be quite intimidating.

Performers who have a lot of confidence can respond aggressively when confronted by an official who gives them full-on eye contact as part of a cautioning procedure. An official wanting to maintain eye contact can reduce the intensity of this perceived assertion by using hand gestures and body movements to minimise any likely aggression. However, maintaining eye contact when talking and listening to a performer or manager normally gives an impression of confidence and honesty, while making little eye contact can be interpreted as dislike.

If officiating takes place outdoors and involves wearing sunglasses or head gear that precludes performers being able to see their eyes, officials should think carefully about the appropriateness of removing their glasses or head gear prior to talking with performers. This shows a sign of respect but also enables them to make more effective use of their eyes. It also ensures that the performer is left in no doubt about the intensity of the official's comments (if appropriate) and ensures the performer knows the official is making eye contact and is interested in fulfilling the officiating role. Finally, blinking can convey messages to performers. Infrequent blinking (if possible) gives an impression of confidence and is less distracting.

Physical Contact

Officials should always be cautious of using tactile contact with performers. With increasing litigiousness in sport, it is best to avoid physical contact where possible as an official, except in sports where it is part of the role (eg boxing).

Summary

Language is a powerful tool. Officials must use language but they must use it judiciously and in varied forms. The varied use of communication styles will improve an official's officiating capacity. Effective communication will enable officials to control volatile situations, minimise the likelihood of conflict and ensure performers can produce the best spectacle for those watching the game. Officials can use language to make them appear confident, powerful, trustworthy, authoritarian or sympathetic. They should also try to interpret the intentions of performers (and managers, other officials and assessors) through the language they use.

Communication

Officials should:

- develop an acceptable style of communication
- make use of a variety of communication styles
- allow their personalities to come through where appropriate
- monitor their use of communication (eg through video recording).

Chapter 3

Managing Environments and Spectators

Environments

Sports officials can come into contact with a wide range of environments, depending on the sport for which they are officiating. However, most officials will know and understand their officiating space well, regardless of the setting, as the dimensions, minimum requirements and physical spaces are likely to be very similar. For example, a football official will normally operate on a grass pitch, which may be exposed to weather conditions. This presents particular challenges, which will be different for each match. A squash official will always officiate indoors, over a court, which is 23 feet by 32 feet. This consistency of environment is likely to result in limited variation between performances based on venue; however, there are many other aspects of the environment that will impact on the performances of performers, coaches, officials and spectators. Other sports will, by their very natures, have enormously varied competitive environments, where officials have to be sensitive to the variations and need to understand how to present the professional, impartial and objective maintenance of rules/laws and standards. Such sports include motor racing, athletics, sailing and road cycling. In these sports, officials will find themselves overseeing their sport in varied environments in which the consistency of judgement can be affected by the conditions in which they have to officiate.

However, regardless of the environment, sensible officials will prepare in a consistent way. This will mean having a well-formulated pre-performance (and performance and post-performance) routine that enables them to focus on the key issues, rehearse the likely concerns and prepare for the competition to allow the best spectacle, the fairest competition and the safest of outcomes.

When an official arrives at a new venue, there are some basic principles that can be instigated to minimise the risk of environment-related issues affecting the performance.

These include:

- inspecting the ground or playing surface
- checking the security arrangements and evacuation procedures, especially fire safety

- ensuring that equipment is new where necessary, ready and fit for purpose and that appropriate spares are available
- speaking with the managers, captains or performers before the event begins to outline any rule or venue changes, or any minimum expectations the official might have related to the venue (eg in tight football grounds where the sideline is close to the spectators, away teams are often asked not to celebrate goals too close to the sideline for fear of inciting aggression)
- checking technology that might be used as part of the officiating role (eg video technology, ear pieces, arm bands).

A normal reaction for anyone faced with new or unfamiliar surroundings can be a sense of urgency, anxiety or stress. Officials in all sports should ensure they are fully aware of a competition venue and its idiosyncrasies before they begin their officiating role at the event. For example, it would be sensible and appropriate for an official in sailing to have covered the course prior to the race start, to be familiar with the weather conditions and to be aware of safety procedures in the event of a mishap. Officials in charge of major sporting events with significant numbers of fee-paying spectators must also ensure they have appropriate awareness of evacuation procedures, support structures and clear thinking about what would constitute the need to halt, abandon or prevent play from taking place. This would include the approved procedures should power fail and lights no longer be available for the event. This has implications for performer safety but also for spectators at large-scale events such as day/night cricket, netball or night football.

All officials must be acutely aware of the varied conditions in which they may find themselves officiating. Principal concerns for all officials must be the health and safety of the performers and the safety of the environment. Adverse weather conditions will sometimes determine whether or not an event will be held. In cricket, the state of the wicket and the outfield are determinant factors that may prevent a match being started. These conditions are normally a consequence of too much rain producing a water-logged pitch or leaving the outer surfaces with too much surface water for safety to the performers to be guaranteed. In fact, all outdoor sports can be affected by rain and officials in football, athletics, tennis and rugby have postponed matches based on inappropriate playing surfaces due to water presence. When officials take this action to abandon (or postpone) an event, they must remain sensitive to the implications this has on others. Significant others include the spectators (most likely to be paying if observing large-scale professional sport), the transport industries that will have assisted in getting spectators there and now might have to assist in getting them away earlier than expected, and the police or security services being used to manage spectators and assist in the dispersion of them after events. Clearly, issues related to refunds etc are not the responsibility of officials. However, it would be inappropriate of officials not to be sensitive to any concerns that might be angrily aimed at them upon their departure from a venue after having delayed, abandoned or postponed an event.

Perhaps the ultimate responsibility of any official is to uphold the rules/laws of the game and maintain performer safety. Their management role lies firmly within these limitations. However, the role will naturally extend beyond these to involve interaction with others and the need to express themselves in other areas: for example, the tennis umpire who asks the spectators to be quiet during play, the fourth official in football who tries to control activity in the technical area or the cricket umpire who allows time for a bird injured by a ball to be taken from the field.

Another aspect of the environment that officials have to manage is the increasing interest and use of technology in the decision-making process. Some sports have now engaged the use of technology to replace the official (eg the use of Cyclops in tennis to determine whether a service is in or out). In cricket, video technology is now used to assist umpires with decisions that they feel they are not well placed to correctly judge (eg run-out decisions). In rugby league, officials are now wired for sound – to allow spectators to hear the commentary and constant performer–management communication used throughout the match – but they also have an earpiece to make use of video technology on difficult decisions. In other sports, technology has yet to be used in an official capacity but is used by the media companies to highlight potential mistakes by officials (eg football and goal-line decisions). How officials make the best use of technology is partly dependent on the rules/laws regulating the game and the access to such support that the governing body will allow.

With the increasing amounts of money involved in sport, much closer scrutiny of performer preparation is given by national and international governing bodies. The much wider use of drug testing has brought new demands on performers and officials in sport.

With the advent of professional officials, and even where officials are still voluntary, assessment of officials' performances is often overseen by an independent assessor. If an official is to manage the environment effectively, an awareness of the preference of an assessor is quite useful. Clearly, assessors have a key role to play but they often have preferred styles they like to see. While officials may be unable to *change their spots*, it may be relevant for minor adjustments in officiating behaviour and approach to take account of that expectation. For example, some assessors will prefer to see officials prevent explosive situations, while others may prefer to see how an official manages an explosive situation. Regardless of this, officials must remain calm and must not allow intimidation (from performers, assessors, coaches or spectators) to affect their performance.

The responsibility for controlling restricted areas also falls to the official in many sports. In football, the technical zone is the preserve of managers and performers being substituted and the fourth official will normally oversee this. In the case of swimming, part of the poolside will be a restricted area that officials will normally patrol. In athletics, prior to an individual's event, athletes' and coaches' access to the competition area may be restricted. It is generally sensible for officials to take a preventative approach to these aspects of their role. By thoroughly preparing and making no assumptions about what performers and support staff understand, officials will minimise such concerns. A simple pre-performance explanation to those involved in the event can save considerable angst later when trying to manage environments properly.

Spectators

As sport has expanded over the years, sports developers have sought to have larger stadia to enable greater enjoyment of the games by more people. In the UK, a typical football stadium will hold in excess of 40,000 people. In tennis, it is not uncommon to seat up to 15,000 fans at a game. Rugby will often have 50,000 spectators and motor sport can have over 200,000 spectators. Clearly, seeing large numbers of people watching sport can be most enjoyable, adding to the spectacle of the event and giving great support to the performers; however, it can also lead to potential for conflict. The responsibility for spectator control rests with a variety of personnel and this does include the official. Part of an official's role must be to ensure that, during the contest, appropriate provision has been made to allow the performers to commit themselves fully to their role and play the game fairly. Sports officials must take the lead in ensuring the safety of the performers and associated staff (coaches, managers, physios etc) but also the public who paid (or not) to watch the event.

While the management of spectators is a role that is clearly multifaceted and requires support from security staff, police and stewards, officials will have considerable power of influence once the game commences. For example, should spectator trouble arise during a match, the official must make decisions regarding the safety of the performers by determining whether the match should continue.

Additionally, the decisions that an official makes can incite unrest within the spectators. Officials must be certain that they do not compromise their authority, vary their decisions or be adversely affected by spectator reaction but, at the same time, they must be sensitive to the interpretation of their decisions by spectators who will often lack impartiality and fail to understand the decision-making processes that leads to official judgements.

The exact nature of the role an official will have in managing spectators will vary considerably between sports; however, it is incumbent upon an official to ensure that the performers' safety, welfare, ability to perform at their highest level and enjoyment is not compromised by spectators' behaviour. On that basis, regardless of what the rules/laws of the game state, the official must exercise control over disruptive, inappropriate or dangerous circumstances propagated by spectators.

It is generally considered appropriate to avoid all contact with spectators during competition. With officials in many sports now becoming quite recognisable (eg Collina is very well known in football throughout the world), sometimes they are as sought after for autographs and general interest stories as some performers. However, when the contest begins, it is inadvisable to cross the barrier between spectator and official. Many fans can gain considerable enjoyment from annoying officials or rattling their cages. This is a common pastime of spectators, coaches and managers towards assistant referees in football. The best avoidance tactic is to minimise eye contact with spectators so as to imply you are not affected by their chants, requests, questions or comments.

Should spectators begin to adversely affect an opposing team with comments that are racist or abusive, officials should intervene and either deal directly with the offending person(s) or, in large spectator venues/sports, engage the appropriate authorities. Similarly, should spectators begin to throw items onto the playing area that might injure performers, officials must take action to have such individuals removed from the venue.

Spectators have no place on the playing area of any sporting event. This presents a danger, not only to the performers, officials and game management staff but also to the spectators themselves. Spectators who insist on entering the playing area must expect to have themselves removed. In the 1970s and 80s, when streaking was quite common at a variety of sporting events, it would usually result in these people being evicted from the ground, charged with an offence and, sometimes, prevented from attending matches in the future. In situations where spectators enter the playing area, officials should take immediate action to stop play, ensure the safety of the performers and guarantee the removal of the offender(s) by stewards, police or other game management staff.

In some sports, animals or birds may enter the playing area. In the Six Nations Championship for Rugby Union, the French supporters may carry cockerels with them to matches. These are often released during the match and sometimes enter the playing area. In such circumstances, officials must make a judgement related to performer safety and possibly to the animal also. If any of these situations becomes extreme, it is advisable to remove performers and take them to the safety and security of the changing rooms, where the public will not normally have access. Clearly, in small-scale events, weekend sport or amateur games, such reactions may be overprotective; however, the underlying principles must remain the same.

Impact of Spectators on Officiating Performance

Studies in the UK have shown what appears to be a significant home advantage for football teams. The basis behind this is far less clear. Spectators in English football are segregated by the team they support. Plus, the home teams always have larger spectator allocations, hence the bias towards home advantage remains a relatively poorly understood concept.

However, speculation has raged that the basis for this bias could lie with the official. That is, since larger spectator allocations are usually made to home teams, it could result in the official being influenced more by home spectator reaction and giving more decisions to the home side. While research shows that spectator reaction can influence decisions from lower-level officials in football, there is no solid basis to assume this also occurs with officials in professional leagues. However, an awareness of the impact that spectator reaction can have is a useful starting point for any official who wants to remain impartial and give the correct, credible and appropriate decisions regardless of the team. Most officials have been on the receiving end of a barrage of abuse from parents, teachers, coaches or others who have been unhappy with an officiating decision. This may place officials under undue pressure, raising doubts about the accuracy of their decision-making and undermining confidence for subsequent decisions that will arise in the match.

Managing Spectators

Officials should:

- be aware of all aspects of security as they relate to the competition arena

- be conscious that spectators, like performers, can impact on an official's thinking and can influence decisions; officials must work hard to block out the noise, comments and impact that significant others can have on their impartial approach to the officiating role

- constantly review their performance to ensure decisions are based on rules/laws and that any subjectivity in decision-making is minimised.

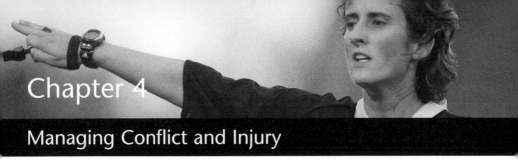

Chapter 4

Managing Conflict and Injury

Conflict

Being an official in any sport will often bring officials into contact with conflict. As the responsibility for maintaining control rests with the official, conflict management will be a fundamental part of the officiating role. To assume these skills are innate and do not require development is naïve and inappropriate. Some officials will be more capable than others of controlling conflict situations; however, to be the best that they can be will necessitate working with others, perhaps attending courses and certainly observing the skills other officials demonstrate in both minimising and controlling conflict situations.

What Causes Conflict?

An understanding of conflict and why it arises in sport is useful to provide context. Most sporting contests will provide a political dimension to life, allowing performers to be involved in competition embedded with:

- tensions
- conflicts
- group struggles
- emergent social problems.

Conflict in sport will arise from a variety of circumstances: some that are controllable and others that are more difficult for the official to prevent. However, the basis is often common and could be a result of:

- poorly delivered instructions
- differing performer objectives
- bad communication
- poor decisions.

Conflict will be heightened when performers (or teams) possess differing goals, demonstrate a high level of interdependence or vary their perceptions. In most sporting conflict situations, performers are likely to become defensive, even though they may be victims themselves. This is because sport can often be described as a form of combat. Many team sports involve the invasion of territory; other sports require performers to invade personal space; most are a form of controlled combat.

The word *conflict* comes from the Latin word meaning *to strike together*. Sporting situations provide cauldrons where incompatible activities, feelings or intentions occur together and are likely to result in some form of conflict. The conflict may be internal, between two or more people, or between large groups of people. It can involve actual confrontation or merely symbolism resulting from words and deeds. Conflict is likely to be expressed through verbal defamation, accusations, threats and physical violence to persons or property. Conflict can remain unexpressed, as in avoidance and denial. However, in such situations, frustration can build and tempers can fray.

A key skill that distinguishes effectiveness between officials will be their ability to resolve conflict when it arises or minimise the potential for it to arise in the first instance. Clearly, conflict can be the result of performer–performer interaction or it can arise from some external influence, which includes the official, spectator interference, coach/manager or the media.

Typical settings in which officials may be required to resolve conflict may include more than just the competition they officiate. Additional situations and personnel with whom conflict can arise include:

- **parents** – this is more likely to occur at junior level, where overzealous parents have an opinion on the game, the coach and the official. This can be ugly at times and may necessitate the removal of parents from the viewing areas

- **performers** – performers are the normal source of conflict. This takes many forms and is often between performers themselves but can include conflict between performers and officials, especially if performers have difficulty with accepting authority or taking responsibility for their actions

- **administrators** – this is more difficult to quantify but sports administrators will sometimes try to gain access to officials and have a role in influencing their thinking. This will usually arise outside the direct competitive environment
- **coaches and managers** – it is not uncommon for coaches to be quite aggressive towards officials in the early part of a game as they try to pressure the official into making errors or becoming wary of decisions against their team. This may take the form of a constant barrage of abuse directed at the official to intimidate, and is often designed to gain a mental advantage.

Conflict with coaches is a special case. Jack Pardee, Houston Oilers Coach, once said: 'A coach spends his entire life thinking he's *fighting off alligators*. An official is just another alligator'. This gives clarity to the adversarial relationship that will exist between coaches and officials, although this is seldom a reciprocal relationship. Most coaches care intensely about their team and its potential to win. They are also likely to possess a built-in bias towards their own team. Officials, however, are less concerned about who wins and should therefore bring objectivity to the process of upholding the rules/laws of the game and should remain impartial throughout the competition.

What is Conflict Resolution?

Conflict resolution in psychology refers to the process of defusing antagonism and reaching agreement between conflicting parties, especially through some form of negotiation. One of the most significant roles that officials undertake is to minimise conflict. However, conflict is part of the sporting environment and, therefore, all officials must possess enhanced skills and diplomacy that will enable them to resolve or control conflict.

Given the nature of sporting contests that bring together highly competitive performers, each desperate to outperform the competition, conflict will often arise due to the tension of the situation, the energy involved and the desire to succeed following the effort invested. In team settings, on the basis that two teams are competing in a sporting contest, conflict is already present. Sports officials, like some managers in corporate settings, may be associated with low levels of trust, similar to police officers or other authority figures. Central to an official's role is handling conflict professionally, quickly and successfully.

England Netball

Recognising Conflict

Conflict will manifest itself in a variety of forms. From performers, it may be poor performance as they seek to control their frustrations. It can sometimes be seen in facial expressions or body language, and officials need to develop early warning systems to identify where potential for conflict may exist. In sports where officials are assessed, assessors will often have a preference to see officials avert the likelihood for conflict to arise, although others are keen to see the skill set that officials can demonstrate in resolving conflict once it has arisen.

In team sports, where the attention of the official will mainly be focused on the action, contact between performers away from the centre of the game can also be a site for conflict. In such situations, assistant officials or even spectators may sometimes have a role in drawing the attention of the official to the incident and the necessary actions. *Paybacks* or retaliation for earlier perceived or real infringement by an opponent are other real sources for conflict and astute officials will record all such incidents and minimise potential retaliatory responses.

Other signs that conflict may be inherent include signals to performers from coaches, repetitive comments made to officials, increased volume in interaction with officials and aggressive body language when performers approach officials to remonstrate or receive disciplinary comments.

Perceptions

A coach storms out of the dugout with arms flailing and voice raised, wanting to confront the official: 'That was a close call and I think you got it right. I'm out here to get those fans in the game and my team going. You made the right call but I want my performers to think I'm out here fighting for them.'

Sometimes, conflict is not conflict. The example above demonstrates what might visually appear to be conflict but which clearly is an example of the coach wanting to *sell* to performers and fans some anger but also to show general support for the officiating decision. While this is likely to occur very seldom in sport, it can happen.

The reverse perceptions are also relevant too. Sometimes, performers can interpret decisions from officials or actions from other performers incorrectly. As a consequence, they make internal judgements (wrongly) and then respond aggressively, sometimes starting a fight, arguing with the official or abusing other performers or officials. The course of action should still be the same; however, it is important to have an understanding of how such situations arise, to minimise their likelihood and to try to calm situations rather than react instinctively and penalise performers immediately.

Avoiding Conflict

Preventative officiating is, in most sports, a preferable style. However, it is not always possible and officials must accept that some conflict will still arise despite their best efforts to prevent it. In an attempt to minimise conflict, it is essential that officials are highly focused on the game and all extraneous thoughts are removed prior to the commencement of competition. By being aware of the performers, the history of the competition, any problem areas or performers, an official can enter the game prepared with powerful knowledge to minimise conflict. Throughout the game, the official must remain objective and make decisions based on the situation that has arisen and how the rules/laws of the game require such events to be judged. An official should never take conflict in competition personally, even if the comments or aggression are directed at them. The official also has the discretion to decide on which actions require a response, discipline or further action and this needs to be in proportion to the flow of the game, the context of the competition and the level of conflict which has arisen. By using positive encouragement and positive body language, an official can minimise conflict in most sporting contests.

Managing Conflict

As part of the building process to improve the conflict skills toolkit, officials need to have considerable internal control over themselves. They should use their presence and:

• be confident
• have a neat, smart, positive appearance and use strong body language
• control their voice and remove emotion
• avoid threats by keeping to the facts and avoiding arguments
• not trivialise but deal with the incident appropriately
• engage with team captains or responsible personnel where appropriate.

Resolving Conflict

Officials must take a controlled approach to the resolution of conflict. Taking a confrontational approach is likely to force performers (or managers) to take sides. If this occurs early in the resolution process, amicable and expeditious solutions are less likely.

Resolving Conflict

While most conflicts will be situation-dependent, guidance to resolving conflict might include:

- not taking sides
- keeping an open mind
- remaining objective
- using other officials where appropriate
- using time valuably
- limiting comment only to the immediate issue.

Levels of Response

Officials should always start off with an appropriate response, avoiding the *bull at a gate* reaction. The preferred first response is a quiet word. If that doesn't work, a louder word might. The next stage would be a very visual warning that is clear to see and provides evidence to the opposition, managers and viewing public that the official has reprimanded the performer and now expects them to control their behaviour and play. Ultimately, dependent upon the sport, the official will have sanctions such as awarding points, penalising performers by moving the centre of play, giving *sin bin* timeouts, producing punishment cards (eg yellow or red as in football) or making a record of the event and dealing with it through a post-match tribunal.

Coping with Conflict

Officials should:

- assume everybody is doing their best to minimise conflict
- accept that conflicts usually arise from technical errors rather than from performers being badly behaved
- acknowledge that conflict may arise when performers feel circumstances have prevented them from playing at their best.

Officials should not:

- assume performers can resolve their own conflict
- allow reputation, aggression, assertiveness or pressure to influence their assessment of conflict in competition
- believe all situations can be determined by them without some negotiation or seeking of alternatives
- assume that performers are the problem
- allow performers to see the outcome as winning or losing.

Injury

Officials will have two perspectives on injury. The first is likely to be a desire to limit occasions when injury might prevent them from officiating at an event. Officials in sports such as football, rugby, netball or hockey, which require officials to have physical mobility and injury-free status similar to that of the performers, are clearly most at risk. Many sports, however, do not require a high level of movement ability for officials and, in such cases, injury is unlikely to affect officiating roles.

In sports where officials must be mobile and where they are full-time paid professionals, injury can bring long-term concerns about future employability and short-term concerns about replacement officials. Some sports, such as football, systematically engage a fourth referee whose role (among other duties) is to serve as a substitute for either the referee or assistant referee should they become injured prior to or during the match. Such concerns for officials can lead to game failure or abandonment. In any sport where an official cannot participate, the event may have to be abandoned. However, it is not uncommon in sport, especially at junior levels, for parents, performers, teachers or onlookers to take over the role of an official when injury or some other circumstances prevent the appointed official from completing the duties. Where this arises, it remains incumbent upon the performers to have some sympathy and respect for those prepared to step in at the last moment, as they are unlikely to be a qualified official, may only have scant knowledge of the rules/laws and could also have an interest in one performer or team, which might compromise their impartiality. In all such circumstances, the health and safety of the performers must remain paramount to the substitute official, while trying to apply the rules/laws correctly. Some sports (eg rugby union, boxing) will have insurance concerns in these circumstances and it would be inappropriate for anyone other than a qualified official to take control of a match.

Injury to a Performer

Perhaps a more common issue for officials managing injury is injury to a performer. Most sports have clear guidance relating to the amount of time that can be used to allow the performer to recover, before being taken from the playing area and having to concede the match. Where the guidelines are unclear, officials should make use of common sense to determine what is appropriate.

Most sports performers will, at some stage during their playing careers, have to reconcile injury and the injury process. Getting injured in sport will often invoke a typical grief response, where performers initially struggle to accept the injury. Typical responses will be denial, followed by anger, which may manifest itself during a game immediately after the injury has occurred. Such responses require quick and careful attention by the official, who must protect the injured performer, prevent others from becoming injured, determine the basis of the injury and ascertain whether anyone should be disciplined for the injury.

Injury is very much a part of sport, with typical injury rates being between 15 and 30 injuries for every 1000 hours of competition. Given this, officials must be acutely aware of what constitutes an injury and how the rules/laws of the game support injured performers. Clearly, in exhibition events, the performers are likely to be more sympathetic but, in professional sport and sport where the prestige of success is high, injury to performers provides potential for an advantage to be gained by the other competitor(s).

In any sport where injury arises, the official is the principal person with responsibility to manage the process successfully. This requires a speedy response to assess the extent of the injury and whether the performer is merely feigning injury to gain time, to allow the team (or themselves) to regroup and compose a new strategy, or whether the injury is real and requires immediate medical attention. Officials should assume the worst when approaching an injured performer. Their guard must be up and their ability to assess acting highly sensitised; however, it would be unprofessional and inappropriate for an official not to assume initially that injury is a concern to the performer and needs to be treated by qualified personnel. Officials must also decide if injury has been self-inflicted, in which case, while the injury is still the main concern, the rules/laws of the game may be less sympathetic to the types of time or leniency given to the injured performer's continued involvement in the competition.

In recent years, new guidelines have also been introduced in most sports to cope with some new concerns. In particular, the treatment of head, neck and back injuries has now been given new status, especially in sports where there may be an increased risk of such injury (eg rugby). New regulations in most sports have also been introduced in relation to blood loss. With an increasing prevalence of HIV/AIDS, hepatitis and other blood-born diseases, sports governing bodies have given much greater power to officials to exclude performers who are bleeding, regardless of where the blood is emanating from. Officials must ensure they are aware of minimum requirements but some common sense principles do apply. Performers losing blood require attention. They should be prevented from continuing in the contest until the blood loss has been stopped, and any clothing or implements that have blood on them should be removed or cleaned prior to the performer re-entering the game.

In some sports, injury may arise from contact with an opponent. Usually, the rules/laws of the game will have a mechanism for dealing with this and officials must ensure they exercise the rules/laws correctly. However, following injury and an allowance of time to be treated or assessed for the injury, injured performers who continue to play are essentially declaring themselves fit to continue and should almost certainly forfeit any further access to timeout or injury time for that injury.

Officials must also be acutely aware of the increasing incidence of litigious claims made as a result of sporting contests. In the case of *Allport v Wilbraham* (2003)[1], a performer sought compensation after a catastrophic injury caused by a scrum collapse. The claim that the official had not applied the laws of the game and, in particular, failed to call the scrum in the sequence of *crouch, pause, engage* was subsequently dismissed. However, it highlights again the importance of ensuring officials are fully qualified, aware of the role and responsibility with which they must exercise their position and fully cognisant of the issues related to injury and the potential aftermath of their actions. Governing bodies should constantly update officials' knowledge and test their understanding of the rules/laws, particularly those that relate to issues such as injury.

For sports in which the competition time is limited, officials will often have a responsibility for managing time and the loss of time through injury. While there are clearly more objective mechanisms to manage the time lost through injury, officials in sports where they also act as timekeepers need to be finely attuned to the timekeeping needs and the development of skills, in order to ensure they don't make errors.

Evidence exists that provides some detail of the likelihood that injury might arise. While it is unlikely that officials will have in-depth or personal awareness of all the competitors, knowledge about personality, life stresses and personal coping resources have been shown to be positively correlated to injury in sport. The basis to this is that performers who have type A personalities have significant life stress and limited coping resources and may be unable to focus adequately on competition. They are more likely to miss danger cues and circumstances during competition that more equipped performers will be attuned to.

In some sports, officials might also have control over exclusion criteria for performers who are unfit (not fit to take the playing area), injured or whose continued involvement in the competition would be considered dangerous as it could endanger them or other competitors adversely. This can of course be in conflict with a coach, who may feel they need their performer to continue in the competition and that, being substituted, taken off or the competition being ended, can indicate that the performer is weak or demonstrates worthlessness in that performer. However, contemporary performers are intelligent and sophisticated and their pride and commitment can sometimes be hazardous to injury. Officials should take a more holistic interest in the welfare of all competitors and should make what they feel are appropriate

[1]Beachcroft Wansbrough (2004) 'Insurance Litigation Alert Catastrophic Injury', http://www.rfu.com/index.cfm/fuseaction/RFUHome.Refereeing_Detail/StoryID/5522

judgements on any performer's ability to compete, without risk to themselves or others in the competition.

Managing Injury

Officials should:

- be acutely aware of first-aid provision and emergency procedures prior to the commencement of competition
- not take risks with injury
- always assume a performer is serious when an injury arises
- know the rules/laws of the game as they relate to injury
- understand the implications on time when injury impacts on a competition.

Sports Foto Preben B. Soborg

Chapter 5

Putting Theory Into Practice

Conclusion

Managing people and situations in sport is never easy. The role of an official is complex, stressful, demanding and will often be highly scrutinised. However, it can also be rewarding and satisfying and can provide a positive alternative to playing for those who have an interest in sport but perhaps no longer wish to be part of the competitive sporting environment.

The demands on officials are different from those of performers but, with an ever-increasing interest in sport, with many sports now operating as multi-million pound industries and with increasing levels of litigation across sport, officials must be highly tuned individuals. This necessitates excellent health (especially eyesight), suitable levels of fitness (sport-dependent), outstanding knowledge of the rules/laws of the game, mental toughness and personality characteristics that enable a personal resilience to abuse. But perhaps the defining characteristic required by all officials is management skills. To be a good official requires an ability to manage performers, spectators, administrators and media. It requires an awareness of conflict and how to resolve it. The modern official will have to oversee complex sporting environments, often being driven by external drivers (especially television). However, to underpin these management skills, officials must have highly developed and sensitised communication skills, be able to empathise with the performers but also capable of presenting a framework in which the competition boundaries for acceptable behaviour can be adequately managed to provide all competitors the opportunity of performing at their best.

Officials in all sports should constantly be updating their knowledge. An official should never assume that nothing else can be learned. Watching others, talking about the role, reading about the rules/laws will always give officials who are hungry for development the opportunity to enhance their skills. The motivational and goal-setting needs of any official should be no different from those of a performer. Short- and long-term goals will help to maintain the momentum necessary to improve ability and ensure non-stop progress.

Further Reading

Ali, M., Brookson, S., Bruce, A., Heller, R., Hindle, T. and Langdon, K. (2002) *The Management Book*. London: Dorling Kindersley Ltd. ISBN: 0-7513-6968-3.

Collina, P. (2003) *The Rules of the Game*. London: Pan Macmillan Ltd. ISBN: 0-330418-72-6.

Grunska, J. (1999) *Successful Sports Officiating*. Champaign, Illinois: Human Kinetics. ISBN: 0-880117-48-6.

Weinberg, R.S. and Richardson, P.A. (1990) *Psychology of Officiating*. Champaign, Illinois: Human Kinetics. ISBN: 0-880114-00-2.